The Cat Sold It!

Feline Stars of the Advertising World

written and designed by

ALICE L. MUNCASTER &
ELLEN YANOW SAWYER

Photography by Peter Basdeka

CROWN PUBLISHERS, INC.
New York

We dedicated our first book to our
first cats (who "introduced" us).
This book is dedicated to our other cats
so they won't be jealous.

Published by Crown Publishers, Inc., 225 Park Avenue South, New York, New York 10003, and represented in Canada by the Canadian MANDA Group
CROWN is a trademark of Crown Publishers, Inc.

Manufactured in Hong Kong

Library of Congress Cataloging-in-Publication Data
Muncaster, Alice L.
The cat sold it!

1. Cats in advertising. I. Sawyer, Ellen Yanow.
II. Title.
HF5827.M87   1986   659.1'96368'009   86–4484
ISBN 0–517–56303–7

10   9   8   7   6   5   4   3   2

COVER AND TITLE PAGE ILLUSTRATION: Belding Heminway Company, Inc.
The kitten is an active trademark of Belding Heminway Company, Inc.

Feline Stars of the Advertising World

magine, for a moment, that you are a time traveler. Invisible, you're able to fly back to the past (maybe with your pet cat in tow) and see firsthand what living in 1880, 1900, 1925, and 1940 was really like. Then, when you return safely to the present, you'll have a new perspective on history—that subject we usually think of as nothing but a boring memorization of dates and names.

You'll be surprised, we think, to discover that cats have not only been beloved companions to cat lovers during your time trip but have also been important to the development of national and international commerce! Wherever you pause in your journey, you'll see cats used in advertising. In fact, they're some of the real stars of the advertising world and have been pictured in almost every possible kind of advertising.

About a dozen years ago, we started finding clues that eventually led to the discovery of these feline celebrities. Because we like cats (although that is not a prerequisite for you to

The artists who created early advertising trade cards cleverly drew the products into the card's illustration. But sometimes you had to look rather closely to see it. In this 1880s card, a thread spool was made into a drum and the strings of the bass fiddle were made of thread. Jonas Brook & Bros., Limited, began doing business in the United States in the late 1800s, but the company's roots date back to the 1840s in England.

Children were supposed to be well-behaved and well-dressed in turn-of-the-century America, and this early die-cut (shaped) advertising calendar top shows a Victorian artist's portrayal of the perfect little boy. Of course, mothers didn't always dress their sons this way in the late 1800s, but some of these modified sailor-boy outfits were still being seen in the early 1920s. Cats were often included in Victorian art because family pets were important members of the household.

join us in this adventure) we began noticing that cats appeared in the ads in old magazines. We saw a cat with a strange medicinal tonic in an ad from the 1890s. There was another in a soap ad.

We began a special mission back then—and it was successful. We wanted to determine just how widespread the involvement of cats in advertising really was. So we looked at stacks of old sheet music and found a cat here and there posing on the covers. Occasionally one turned up on the colorful box of a child's game. Some fabulous felines greeted us from magazine covers, posters, and signs. Sometimes we found them on bottle or box labels, sometimes on cartons or tin containers.

We were hooked. We became detectives, determined to find more of these purr-fectly wonderful persuaders. And if you join us in a look at the past, you'll see what we found— cats endorsing everything from household cleaners to sewing thread, newspapers and magazines to cigars and cigarettes, theater productions to whiskey and wine, breakfast cereal to fountain pens, blankets to perfume, ice cream to Christmas gift catalogs, candy to cat food.

If you like cats, you can understand why the people who are responsible for selling goods have so often turned to the cat for help. There's no doubt about it—cats are eye-catching. They're interesting to watch. They're cute and curious. Sometimes they act silly, mysterious, or regal. And they add pizzazz to ads, making a product look better than its competition, even if both products are basically the same.

In our first book, *The Cat Made Me Buy It!*, we focused on cats from the pre-television era of advertising. Now we've gone beyond that, to show you more cats—including the ones that dazzle audiences today. But the advertising you'll see, along with these furry spokescats, will be better appreciated if you try to imagine yourself back in the times when the ads were created.

The invitation is open. All it takes is a little imagination on your part. Think of every cat you see as a cat of the present because YOU ARE THERE—an observer of life around you in Victorian times, the pre-World War I years, the Roaring Twenties, the Great Depression and World War II era, the fifties, sixties, seventies, and eighties. It's really not difficult. We've provided a short guide for your tour and an explanation of each picture along the way. The rest is up to you. . . .

Early American manufacturers often provided retailers with small colorful advertising cards, which were given away to customers. The Northwestern Soap Company distributed a series of cards picturing the Three Little Kittens from the popular children's story to promote its White Cross soap. Shown at right is the first card of the series.

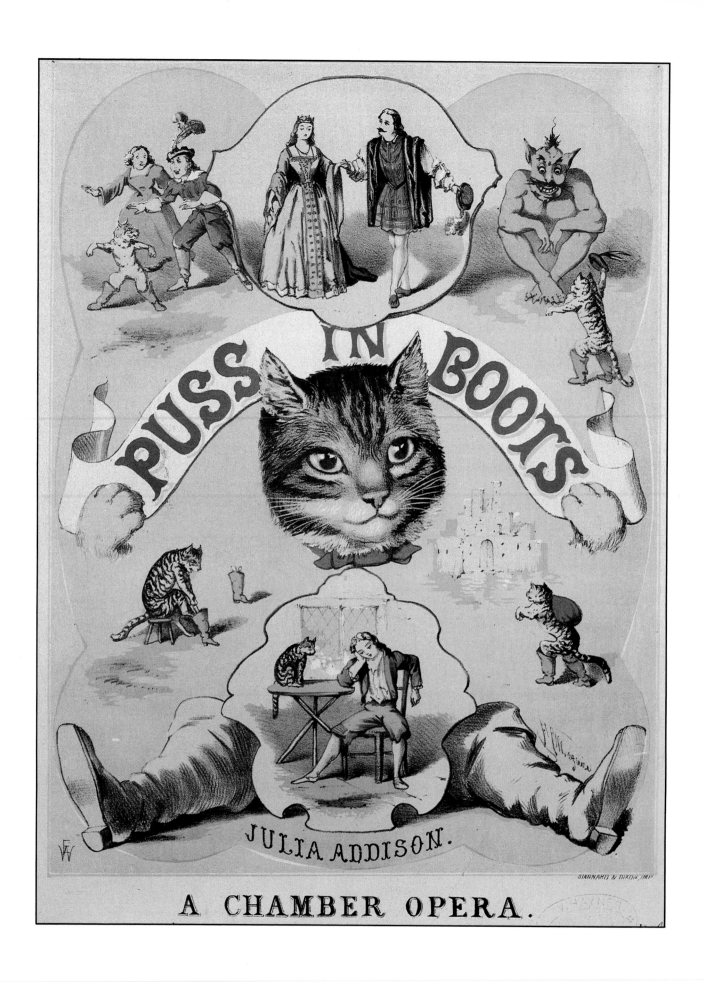

PUSS IN BOOTS

JULIA ADDISON.

A CHAMBER OPERA.

The Late Nineteenth Century

ll around you, America is booming. In the future, people will call this the time of the Industrial Revolution, but everyone now just calls it "progress." The year is 1899.

As you take a trip into town from the farm, you notice how the ladies are careful not to let their skirt hems drag in the mud along Main Street. Many of the gentlemen you see from your seat in the horse-drawn wagon have handlebar mustaches, and you pass several saloons and "men's clubs" where a strange new music called "ragtime" is being played on the piano.

Business is growing so fast it's changing America almost daily. Factories, manned by large numbers of immigrants from Europe, are seemingly everywhere, and these families are bringing new customs to your town. The railroads that now link East and West have ended the era of the stagecoach forever.

At the general store, you receive a small card picturing a beautifully colored illustration of a cat with a spool of thread. In the past few years, lithography companies have sold millions of these advertising cards to manufacturers and storekeepers, who gave them away to their customers. You'll take yours home and paste it in your scrapbook, as everyone else does. It's remarkable that these cards have brought colorful art into most American homes for the first time.

There are so many new inventions these days—typewriters, telephones, and "horseless carriages." One of your fondest memories is that of attending the fantastic World's Fair in Chicago in 1893. You smile as you think that finally cowboys and Indians are becoming more civilized. The nation's attention recently has turned to reports of the Spanish-American War instead of the escapades of Wild West outlaws.

From here, you look forward to that once-in-a-lifetime experience—"the turn of the century." The Victorian era is drawing to a close as Queen Victoria nears the end of her reign in England. Your family pet—a cat, of course—can only look at you questioningly as you daydream about the marvelous things that must surely lie ahead in the long-awaited twentieth century.

"Puss in Boots," the story of a brilliant cat that wins fame and fortune—not to mention a beautiful bride—for his master, is documented as early as 1697 when Charles Perrault wrote *Le Chat Botté*. This beautiful cover from a piece of British sheet music shows several scenes from the story. Chamber operas such as this one from 1868 were intended for performance by a small orchestra in intimate surroundings—in contrast to more classic, longer operas.

Competition was fierce among the manufacturers of early children's games and puzzles. If one company came up with a good idea, another soon adapted it. So it is not surprising to find cat bandit puzzles from both McLoughlin Brothers of New York (Magic Picture Puzzles—1893), shown above, and from Parker Brothers of Salem, Massachusetts (Robber Kitten Picture Puzzle—late 1890s), at the bottom of page 9. McLoughlin Brothers was the first and largest publisher of children's books in America, and became quite well known for the exceptionally beautiful illustrations found on its books, puzzles, games, and paper dolls. The company was started in 1828 by John McLoughlin and was sold to a competitor in 1920.

George S. Parker began producing games in the early 1880s and named his company Parker Brothers when he convinced his brother to join in the venture in 1888. The company has created over a thousand different games since its inception and it still flourishes. Shown at the top of page 9 is the box lid of another popular Parker Brothers game sold from 1899 to 1904. The illustration was also used on a puzzle in the Robber Kitten puzzle box.

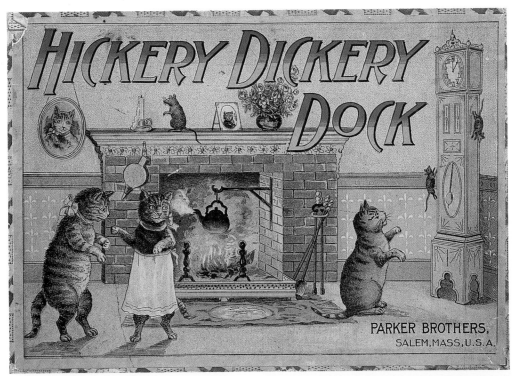

Maine coon cats are exotic-looking longhaired felines that are considered by cat fanciers to be America's first native breed of cat. The Michigan Stove Company of Detroit featured "Garland" (a "coon" cat named for its popular stove brand) on this turn-of-the-century advertising card. Coal- and wood-burning stoves used for cooking and heating during this era often were decorated with intricate nickel-plated Art Nouveau designs—no doubt to appeal to the women who spent a good portion of their lives using them in the kitchen. The Michigan Stove Company dates back to 1864 and, at one time, it was considered the largest manufacturer of stoves and ranges in the world. The company was sold to the Welbilt Corporation in 1955.

Just about every youngster has played tiddledywinks at one time or another but, in 1892, some lucky children received the game box shown at right—a most outstanding version of the game. It was made by McLoughlin Brothers of New York. The cats on the box lid also stand watch inside and players must flip tiny plastic disks through their open mouths to score points.

"Don't Tommy, Don't!"

The Great Atlantic and Pacific Tea Company used the back of this die-cut card to advertise its 135 stores in 1883. The first of its stores opened in 1859 as a discount shop, selling tea bought directly from clipper ships docked in New York City's harbor. The company was the first to develop private label foods ("house brands") in the 1880s and, in the 1920s, was the first to make prepackaged cuts of meat available at self-service meat counters. Today there are over a thousand A&P supermarkets nationwide.

"Little Charles" was a print given free to subscribers of *The Home,* a monthly magazine published in Cleveland, Ohio, by S. L. and Frederick Thorpe. Begun in 1874, it carried both nonfiction and short stories until it was merged in 1878 with another Thorpe monthly for children and renamed *Home Companion: A Monthly for Young People.* That publication eventually became *Woman's Home Companion* (1897–1957), one of the most prominent early women's magazines. "Little Charles" was printed by Haskell and Allen, a Boston lithography company that produced art prints in the style of Currier and Ives. Never a serious contender in the competitive printmaking business, the firm closed in 1875 after just four years of production.

PUBLISHED BY HASKELL & ALLEN, 61 HANOVER ST. BOSTON, MASS.

LITTLE CHARLES

GIVEN AWAY TO EVERY SUBSCRIBER TO THE "HOME."

Published at Cleveland, Ohio, at 50 Cents per Year, Postage Paid.

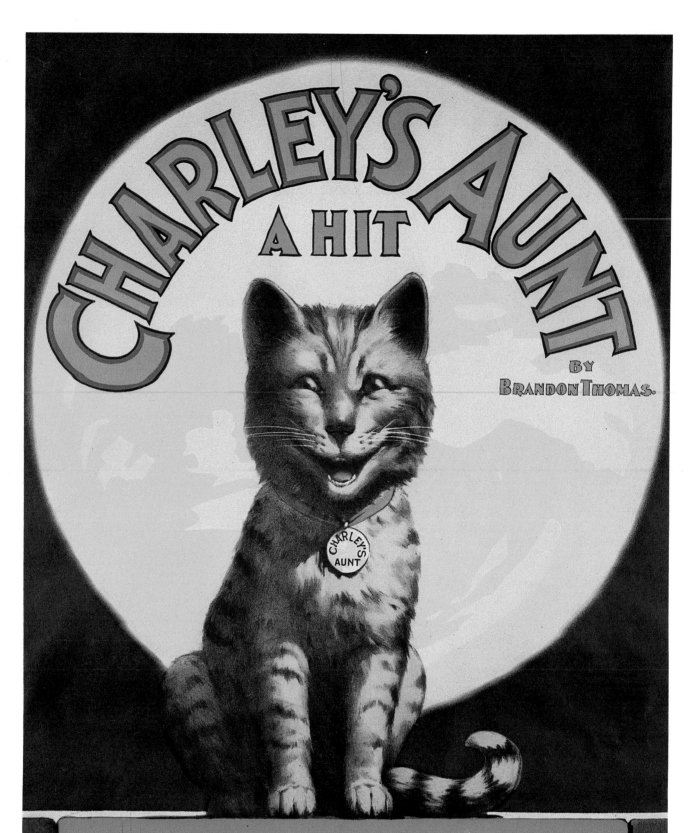

The "Old Tom" of Old Tom Gin came to life on this advertising card dated October 1885. It announced the appointment of Du Vivier & Co. of New York as U.S. agent for Boord & Son Ltd. Old Tom was a sweet gin that was popular in the late nineteenth century and, one legend says, was named for a cat. Boord & Son dates back to 1866 in London. They began their own U.S. operations for the sale of gin and vodka in 1935.

Charley's Aunt was a classic Victorian farce—a three-act comedy by British actor and playwright Brandon Thomas (1856–1914). The plot, which doesn't involve a cat, revolves around two college students (Jack and Charley) who invite their sweethearts to their rooms during a special college weekend to meet Charley's aunt from Brazil. When the aunt is delayed, another boy impersonates the aunt by donning a feminine costume. Then the real aunt arrives! The play was first performed at the Royalty Theatre in London in December 1892. This poster, which measures 27″ x 36″, was used in Massachusetts for a later production (ca. 1895–1900). The play has been made into a number of movies in at least three countries—the most memorable being a 1925 version starring British comedian Syd Chaplin (the older brother of American comedy star Charlie Chaplin).

Black Cat Whiskey was an important product of Ullman, Einstein & Co., Cleveland, Ohio. The firm dates to 1881, and the Black Cat brand—a blended whiskey—was introduced in 1898. The company was dissolved after 1919, when the 18th Amendment to the U.S. Constitution prohibited the manufacturing and selling of alcoholic beverages.

"Cheese it!" was a slang expression in the late 1800s which meant "Look out!" (as in "Cheese it, the cops!"). The Schumacher and Ettinger Co. printed this Cheese It! cigar label design and offered it to cigar manufacturers and retailers for use on cigar boxes. The design is from before 1892, when the prominent New York lithography house was merged into the American Lithographic Company. Shown here is a card from a salesman's sample book, offering the labels with or without the Cheese It! name imprinted at $20 per thousand—two cents each.

The Catlin Tobacco Company, founded in 1840 by Daniel Catlin, produced cigar, pipe, and cigarette tobacco in St. Louis until it was sold to the American Tobacco Company in 1898. The cat and kittens shown in the sign appeared on the company's advertising in the 1880s and 1890s and were apparently intended to create an association in the minds of consumers between the interesting felines and the company name. Because meerschaum pipes were known to be expensive pipes of the highest quality, Catlin probably named this tobacco Meerschaum—and pictured such pipes on its boxes and packages —to imply that the tobacco also was of a premium quality.

Games of chance have always intrigued people—and the game of Lotto has enjoyed success for nearly a century. This version of the game was produced by McLoughlin Brothers of New York, one of the largest producers of beautifully colored children's books and games during the Victorian era.

Cats in hats brought the advertising message to life for Leopold Mendel and I. W. Gosling, wholesale distributors of hats, on this 1894 calendar. Such calendars were often given away to storekeepers to keep a manufacturer's or jobber's name in view—a practice still used by companies today. Jacob Redford was a traveling salesman for Mendel, Gosling & Co.

Everything from diamonds to eyeglasses could be bought at a jewelry shop in the late 1880s. The Spencer Optical Manufacturing Company of New York City promoted its line of Audemaier opera glasses to jewelers in the East and Midwest with a series of advertising cards featuring animals—including cats—around 1888–90. The company began using the Audemaier name in 1885 and, besides eyeglasses, sold magnifiers, field glasses, and telescopes.

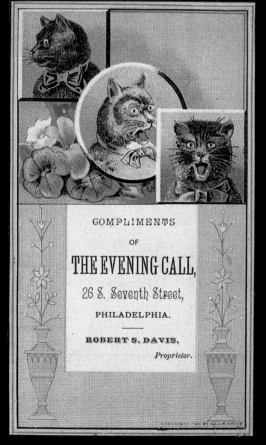

Top left: Advertising cards of the 1880s were used to promote almost every type of product imaginable. This card is one of a series produced in 1883 by Donaldson Brothers Lithographers of New York City to promote Clark's thread. Cats were often associated with thread in early advertising, probably because cats have always enjoyed playing with thread and thread spools. *Bottom left: The Evening Call* was a newspaper published from 1883 to 1900, and the back of the card shown here announces an open-air concert of the Evening Call Band, described as the largest brass band ever organized in Philadelphia. The owners of the paper sponsored the concert, which was held two days before publication of the newspaper actually began, to stimulate readership.

Tabby cats come in a variety of brown and gray colors, their bold stripes distinguishing them from their many feline cousins. It's anyone's guess why the Chappell & Co. sheet music cover shown at the right pictured three tabbies—or why the lively dance tune was named for them in the first place. Polkas were developed in Bohemia in the early 1800s, but this music is from the latter part of the century. Chappell has been actively publishing music in Great Britain since 1811.

TABBY POLKA

By

P. BUCALOSSI

COMPOSER OF MERRY FOOTSTEPS, P&O POLKA.
LONDON; CHAPPELL & Cº 50 NEW BOND Sᵗ

ENT. STA. HALL.

PRICE	
DUET	4-
ORCHESTRA	4-
SEPTETT	2-
	1-

Lithographers printed several different sizes of cigar box labels in the late 1800s and early 1900s. Designs were available either already titled or untitled, so they could be customized for a cigar manufacturer or large retail outlet. *Above:* The *Catchy* label is from an 1895 sample book used by salesmen for the O. L. Schwencke Company, New York. It could only be used for medium-brown color cigars, because the word "Colorado" on the label refers to that color of tobacco. This type of rectangular label was affixed to the inside lid of the cigar box by the box maker.

Two other examples of "inner" lid labels are *House Friend,* printed by Witsch and Schmidt, New York (ca. 1892), before they became affiliated with the American Lithographic Company, and *Mischief,* by George Waldkoenig, Baltimore, Maryland (ca. 1906). Smaller "end" labels were used on the outside of the box after cigars were packed at the cigar factory—such as the 1909 *Tom & Dick* label from H. F. Martin of York, Pennsylvania. It shows the rich embossing and "bronzing" popular at the beginning of this century.

HOUSE FRIEND

TRADE MARK, LITH. BY WITSCH & SCHMITT 84 BOWERY,N.Y.

MISCHIEF

Cats took a trolley ride and put the dogs to work on this intricately die-cut calendar top from the late 1880s or 1890s. The actual size of this exceptionally fine example of Victorian promotional advertising is 8½″ x 14″.

These two cute kittens were created by J. H. Bufford's Sons, a Boston lithography company, and the 7″ x 8½″ cardboard die-cut was sold to New England manufacturers as an advertising giveaway piece in the mid- to late 1800s. The company was well known for its highly detailed designs until its demise in 1890. One man who took advantage of this sales stimulator was Charles H. Richardson of Newburyport, Massachusetts. He began producing cough drops in 1863, while much of the nation was engaged in the Civil War. The cough drops were sold throughout New England, but Richardson achieved greater success as a candy manufacturer and grocer from 1876 until his death in 1933.

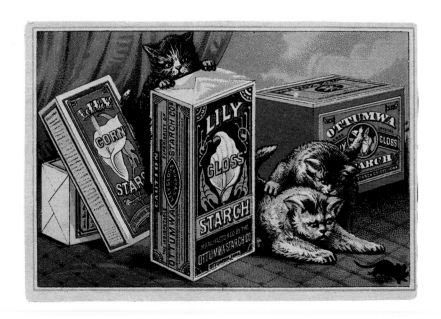

Soapine was a washing product used by housewives in the 1800s. It was made by the Kendall Manufacturing Company of Providence, Rhode Island, a prominent American company founded in 1827 by Henry L. Kendall. The colorful card shown above was used in the 1880s, after Kendall's death. The company ceased production in the mid-1930s.

Advertising cards of the 1880s that showed the products being advertised in the illustration were more expensive to produce than cards that just showed pretty pictures (called stock art cards). But many companies felt the investment in customized advertising art was worth the additional expense, as did the Ottumwa Starch Company, which produced Lily Gloss and Lily Corn Starches. Those packages were featured along with cute cats in the card shown here. The Ottumwa Starch Company was owned by the National Starch Manufacturing Company of New York, and operated a factory in Ottumwa, Iowa, from the late 1870s until the 1890s.

Dressmakers and tailors who wanted fine thread around the turn of the century looked to the Cat's Selecta brand. The cat symbol even appeared on the cellophane wrapping of each spool. This Belgian brand was a product of Filature et Filteries Reunies.

These classic Victorian-style cats advertised Hood's Sarsaparilla—a patent medicine made by the C. I. Hood Co. of Lowell, Massachusetts. On the back of this card is a drawing of the company's factory and testimonials from druggists extolling the therapeutic value of sarsaparilla—a combination of roots, herbs, and bark—for supposedly purifying the blood and restoring vigor to those who were tired or ill.

Presented by

GEO. A. PECKHAM,

PROPRIETOR OF

Peckham's
Balsam

Cough and Lung

PROVIDENCE, R. I.

This die-cut cardboard keepsake shows the stunning color and artistic realism that characterized lithography of the late Victorian era. George A. Peckham, a Providence, Rhode Island, druggist, started his extract and essence business in 1870 and traveled the New England countryside selling his patent medicines to other druggists and grocers. His son, George, Jr., carried on the family business after Peckham's death in 1912, but the company ceased production around 1925.

More than seventy-five years ago, this finely lithographed German
calendar probably graced the home of someone who loved cats very
much—and, at the end of 1909, that person carefully packed it away
to ensure its preservation. To check the date, the rose at the left of the
cat's back slides aside to reveal tiny pages of the calendar beneath.

The Pre–World War I Years: 1900–1919

hings you never dreamed could happen did happen in the last two decades. It's 1919, and what you've seen firsthand will make great reading in the history books of the future.

It was easy to keep up on current events—the daily newspaper became the major communications medium that everyone could afford. You read about the first "aeroplane" flight by the Wright brothers at Kitty Hawk in 1903. The papers reported the changing of women's fashions from bustles to the Gibson Girl look—a slim silhouette inspired by the drawings of Charles Dana Gibson. You saw the style of home furnishings and art change from Victorian to flowery Art Nouveau.

In 1900, you might not have believed you could ever see a sky show as spectacular as Halley's comet, but you saw it in 1910. Some people would never have believed that women would be given the vote but, thanks to the Suffragettes, it will become a reality in 1920. And the wildly fraudulent claims of the patent medicine makers were silenced in 1906, after decades of selling "cures" that consisted mostly of alcohol.

But there were sad times, too. A terrible earthquake and fire left San Francisco in ruins in 1906. Two ocean liners sank—the *Titanic* when it struck an iceberg in 1912 and the *Lusitania* when it was hit by a German torpedo in 1915. And the world engaged in its worst war of record, with modern inventions helping to make its devastation worse. For the first time, bombs were dropped from flying machines.

Much of this history has found its way into popular books, music, and plays, but for entertainment you prefer the vaudeville shows with their live comedians. You've also started attending "the movies." Hollywood, where the weather is well suited for outdoor filming, is destined to become the movie capital of the world.

Piano playing is still very much in vogue, too, with families and friends singing along to the popular tunes. The covers of the song sheets you play are very colorful and the illustrations sometimes are of cats (your favorites!).

Now you're optimistic. From here on, you know the world can only get better and better.

THERE'S ALWAYS MORE

CREAM of WHEAT

Painted by George Gibbs for Cream of Wheat Co   Copyright by Cream of Wheat Co.

The illustration on this Cream of Wheat cereal ad was first used in 1907 but was used again in 1920. It is one of a long-running series of ads featuring "Rastus," the chef. The Cream of Wheat Company was founded in 1895 and was a prolific advertiser through the early years of this century when mothers routinely prepared hot breakfasts for their families, including hot cereals such as Cream of Wheat. The company became part of Nabisco Brands, Inc., in 1961, and Cream of Wheat is still produced. The creation of Rastus was inspired by an anonymous waiter in a Chicago restaurant. He was paid $5 to pose for a photograph but, despite many attempts to determine his identity, it remains unknown to this day.

Brightly colored baby chicks illustrated Lewando's French dyers and cleaners' booklets for children—and counter-top change trays—in the early 1900s. A cat served as the "dyemaster." This advertising campaign was created by a New York City theatrical producer, and ads were placed in opera and theater programs to attract the carriage trade. Clothing left for cleaning at any of Lewando's many locations in New England was shipped to the company's main plant in Massachusetts by railroad. It took three to four weeks for the then-complicated wet (French) cleaning process. The firm was established in 1829 and is still doing business today. At the time these booklets and enameled porcelain tray were produced, live baby chicks—dyed various colors with vegetable dye—were displayed at some of Lewando's stores to tie in with the ad campaign.

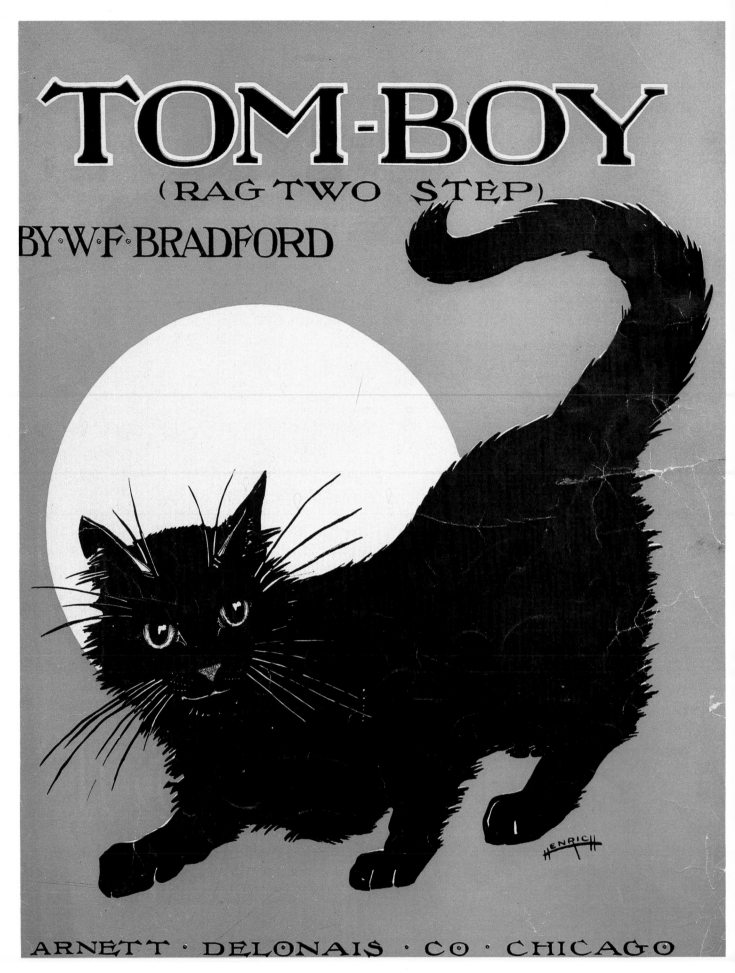

WAMPUS CAT RAG

Words and Music
by
JIMMIE COX

Published by
PACE & HANDY MUSIC CO.
388 BEALE AVE
MEMPHIS, TENN.

When "Wampus Cat Rag" was published in 1918, ragtime music was losing ground to blues and jazz. W. C. Handy, one of the publishers of "Wampus Cat Rag," was a traveling band leader who recognized the potential of this kind of music and became a well-known blues publisher. He even dubbed himself the "Father of the Blues" and gave that title to his autobiography in 1941. Although one definition of wampus cat is "a bloodthirsty beast . . . mean beyond belief," and another is "a foppish clod," the cute cats shown on the cover hardly fit either description. During the teens and the twenties, colloquial use of wampus cat meant "unbeatable" or "jim dandy." Cat enthusiasts would probably vote for the latter definition!

Ragtime music—with its jaunty, syncopated beat—had captured the fancy of America by the time this "Tom-Boy" music sheet was published in 1908. But rags weren't always so popular. They first came on the scene in saloons and houses of ill repute in the 1890s, and Victorian America immediately denounced the music as immoral. It was, however, hard to dislike the upbeat tunes and, until their popularity declined around the end of World War I, a wide variety of subjects—including cats—provided inspiration for composers.

Boston Sunday Post
SUNDAY MAGAZINE

BOSTON, MASS.
APRIL 20, 1913

PART 5
20 PAGES

The Circus Season

SUNDAY MAGAZINE
Of the SUNDAY RECORD-HERALD

PART 3   20 PAGES   CHICAGO, ILLINOIS SEPTEMBER 15, 1907

IN PRAISE OF CATS
By AGNES REPPLIER

"UNCLE JOE" CANNON
ON THE WABASH

Cats just being themselves made good illustrative subjects for the covers of these two pre–World War I Sunday newspaper supplements. Newspapers began including these types of Sunday "magazine" sections around the turn of the century. Within a few years, the Associated Sunday Magazines claimed a circulation of over one million readers in eight different cities by publishing a "generic" magazine customized with the name of each participating paper. Sunday magazines continue to be read by millions of people each weekend.

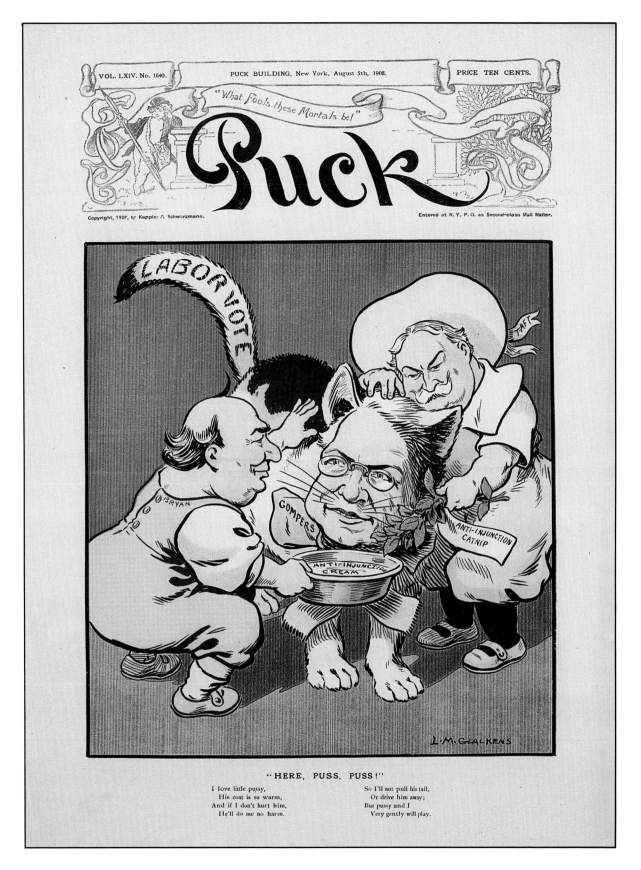

VOL. LXIV. No. 1640. PUCK BUILDING, New York, August 5th, 1908. PRICE TEN CENTS.

"What Fools these Mortals be!"

Puck

Copyright, 1908, by Keppler & Schwarzmann. Entered at N. Y. P. O. as Second-class Mail Matter.

"HERE, PUSS, PUSS!"

I love little pussy,	So I'll not pull his tail,
His coat is so warm,	Or drive him away;
And if I don't hurt him,	But pussy and I
He'll do me no harm.	Very gently will play.

Puck magazine was well known for its political satire during its forty-one years of publication (1877–1918). In this 1908 cover cartoon, the cat represents Samuel Gompers, president of the American Federation of Labor, and the other characters are presidential candidates William Jennings Bryan (Democratic Party) and William Howard Taft (Republican Party). Because Gompers could influence a large number of union members to vote in favor of one candidate or the other, both contenders were depicted as trying to woo the labor vote by offering promises of pro-labor legislation. Taft won the election and served one term as president.

37

Board games were first created in the 1840s. Their themes were moralistic or educational in nature then, but by the time these two games were made, Americans were playing board games just for the fun of it. The Three Little Kittens and The Game of Puss are board games made by the Milton Bradley Company of Springfield, Massachusetts, around 1910–12.

Games of skill have been delighting children and adults for centuries—and this unusual version of ringtoss let players attempt to loop cutout cardboard circles over the head and oversized shoe of a stand-up cat. The colorful costuming of the caricature cat helps date this game to the early 1900s, when musical performers in traveling minstrel shows entertained audiences all over America. This game was produced by the Milton Bradley Company of Springfield, Massachusetts, which still produces games today.

Small pocket mirrors—imprinted with advertising messages on the celluloid side—were popular as giveaways in the early years of the twentieth century. Because the mirrors were useful, they were often kept for many years, with their advertising message being seen again and again. The mirror shown here was a souvenir of the Louisiana Purchase Exposition held in St. Louis in 1904. Like many businessmen in cities where world's fairs were held, Jacob Kolf opened a café and restaurant to serve patrons of the fair. At the time, it was popular for restaurants to advertise separate dining rooms for men and women ("Ladies and Gents"). The Kolf family also owned a local bakery and had a concession at the fairgrounds.

The black cat on the package of Snappy Snaps made the Snappy brand dress fastener stand out among dressmakers' supplies when World War I was in progress. The Vulcanite Manufacturing Company of Lindenhurst, New York, began producing Snappy Snaps in 1917.

When all the cigars were smoked, turn-of-the-century wooden boxes were often saved and used to store small items around the house. This was especially true if the label pictured a favorite subject! This one was decorated in the style known as "tramp art"—covered with small, elaborately carved wood strips. Such woodworking was common in Europe and was brought to America by German and Scandinavian immigrants in the late nineteenth century. As these craftsmen traveled from place to place seeking work, they sold their carvings to support themselves. Most wood used in tramp art carving came from discarded wooden cigar boxes. Luckily, this box was saved and, in turn, became a valued keepsake.

"I no longer write like a cat" is the message on the Gold Starry fountain pen advertising poster (ca. 1915). Gold Starry of Paris, France, created this 37½" x 57½" poster in the large and flamboyant style of French advertising of the early 1900s—and the phrasing is one familiar to all French children. When they have acquired penmanship skills, they are told by their elders that they no longer write with catlike scratchings. Gold Starry had plenty of competition in the pre–World War I European marketplace, and the company was not a major contender against the better-made English and American pens of the era. The company is now out of business, but they left behind this beautiful reminder of their products.

Vibrant color and startlingly realistic detail made Rafael Tuck & Sons of England one of the most successful printing firms of the late nineteenth and early twentieth centuries. These calendars were pretty enough to be kept in view all year and cherished for more than three-quarters of a century after that. Tuck was a German immigrant who first produced fine art prints in his London print and frame shop in 1866. Because the quality of his work was so outstanding, people enthusiastically bought just about anything he produced. Tuck expanded his business to include popular items of the Victorian era—postcards, bookplates, and a wide variety of paper dolls—which were sold in a number of countries and are highly prized by collectors today. Although the firm still exists, much of its heritage was lost when the company's archives and early printing plates were destroyed in a German bombing raid in 1940.

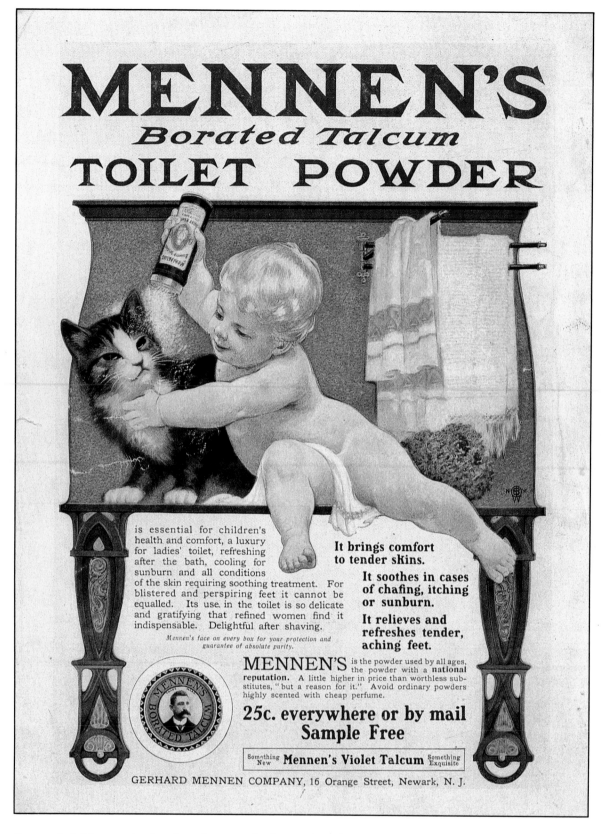

Cats and children make fine friends—mostly due to the tolerance shown by pestered pets! Gerhard Mennen created Borated Talcum Toilet Powder in his New Jersey pharmacy in 1889. By the time this advertisement appeared in the June 1903 issue of *The Delineator,* a popular women's magazine of the time, Mennen was boasting that his product was available "everywhere." Today, the Mennen Company produces a wide range of health and beauty aids, but Borated Talcum Toilet Powder was discontinued in 1931.

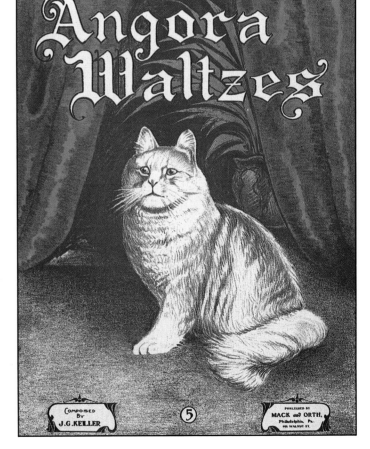

If cats could dance, some would freely cavort to a spritely melody such as the 1910 "Flirtation Caprice"—and some would gracefully whirl around the floor to the strains of the dignified "Angora Waltzes" from 1909. Many pieces of sheet music in this era were created with cats on the covers, and people who know cats are not surprised to discover this. The fluid movements of the feline body —whether stretching after a nap or leaping at a passing butterfly—are truly beautiful enough to inspire musical compositions.

GEO. S. HARRIS & SONS,
CIGAR BOX LABELS AND TRIMMINGS,
718-724 Arch Street, Philadelphia.
BRANCH HOUSES: { S. E. CORNER GRAND AND BOWERY, NEW YORK.
No. 53 STATE STREET, CHICAGO.
No. 4140. $20.00 per 1000. $2.10 per 100.
ALSO FURNISHED BLANK

Even a nickname could become a brand name in the cigar business of the late 1800s and early 1900s. The Kit Kat design and name were first used by George S. Harris and Sons, printers and engravers, before 1892, when the company lost its identity in the merger that created the American Lithographic Company. The Kit Kat name endured, however, and was used by the Joseph Friedman Company of Dayton, Ohio, around 1905.

These free-standing advertising cards served as reminders to purchasers that Globe Polish made it easy to shine metal—in fact, that it turned "work into play"! Globe Polish was originally a paste made in Germany by Fritz Schultz & Co. and produced in England in conjunction with Raimes & Co. of London beginning in 1912. After World War I, the company was purchased by the British firm of Reckitt & Sons Ltd., and today is owned by Reckitt & Colman. Globe Polish was made until 1962.

The Bemis cat-in-the-bag symbol dates back at least to the 1880s, but it is shown here at the right on a celluloid advertising pin-back button from the 1920s, intended for wearing on a collar, lapel, or hat. The button is among the thousands of different types of advertising buttons given away to customers in the first two decades of this century. The Bemis Brothers Company was founded in 1858 and produced bags that were used to package goods in a variety of industries. Companies that bought the bags customized them, of course, but the cat symbol could generally be found imprinted at the top of the bag as shown below on a cloth flour sack. Company stationery and invoices, and even employee service award pins, featured the cat at one time or another. Sadly, Bemis Company, Inc., no longer uses the cat as its corporate symbol.

Before radio and television provided in-home entertainment, people relied on the parlor piano. Little girls by the millions (and a lot of boys, too) learned to play the piano as a required social skill—and many afternoons and evenings were spent with families and friends gathered around the upright or baby grand singing popular tunes. "Pussy A Meowing Musicale" (the sheet music shown at left) was an entertaining melody written in 1908. A musicale is a short program of music forming part of a social occasion. In this piece, all the words are "Me-o-w."

The Twenties and Thirties

ow it's 1939. The last twenty years have been the best and the worst of your life. As you think back, you feel that you've lived a lifetime in just a few short years.

You had some wonderful times in the speakeasies during the Roaring Twenties. Although Prohibition kept people from openly selling liquor, it wasn't hard to find a place where the music was loud, and you danced to live jazz bands or 78-rpm records on the phonograph. Flapper dresses were stylishly short at the knee, and there were some very snazzy cars zipping about town, with exotic names like Pierce-Arrow and Duesenberg.

You were excited when, in 1927, you saw the first movie with sound—*The Jazz Singer,* with Al Jolson. The theater was built to look like a palace, and tiny star lights twinkled in the painted-sky ceiling. You've been there many times—to see movies like *Wings* (the first to win an Academy Award) and, this year, to see the breathtaking *Gone With the Wind.*

No one really thought the crash of the stock market would happen that October Thursday in 1929. You've been lucky. You had a job throughout the Great Depression. But many people you know have been homeless and very poor; the past decade was a hard time for all. Everyone listened to the radio, though—the center of family entertainment. They heard programs like "The Green Hornet" and "Amos 'n Andy." The "Mercury Theatre of the Air" will always be remembered, too, for its Halloween spoof that terrified half the nation in 1938. Its production of the play *War of the Worlds* was so realistic that casual listeners thought they were hearing about a real invasion from Mars! You were pretty scared yourself, and packed up your cat and your suitcase—just in case you needed to make a quick escape!

Love songs and sad songs became classics, from "I Found a Million-Dollar Baby" to "Brother, Can You Spare a Dime?" It seems that money was on everyone's mind.

Now, as 1940 approaches, you desperately hope the United States will stay a nation at peace. People are reading Faulkner, Steinbeck, and your favorite, Fitzgerald. But you love to look at magazines, too, and you notice that advertisements have changed a lot since your grandmother's day. They aren't so old-fashioned-looking anymore. A new age of society is waiting just out of sight.

The delightful cats at the piano showed readers of *Punch* magazine in the 1930s what a brilliant shine Mansion Polish could produce. The ad ran just a month after Chiswick Products Ltd. was created from a corporate merger. Mansion Polish was first sold in 1912 and can still be purchased in England today.

BEFORE THE RECEPTION

Kitten: "I am glad that we live in a good family who use 'MIN' on the piano. It makes such a splendid mirror."

Mother Cat: "Yes, and if you want to see how your tail hangs you have only to look in the floor polished with Mansion Polish."

MANSION POLISH

makes floor polishing so easy. Excellent for stained or Parquet floors and Linoleum. For dark wood use Dark Mansion.

In tins 6d., 10½d. & 1/9. Large household tin containing 2 lbs. nett 3/-.

MIN

the wonder cream of a hundred uses gives a most brilliant finish to the piano. Cleans and polishes White Enamel paint, Glass, China, Japanese Lacquer and all highly polished surfaces.

TINS 6d. and 1/-

If any difficulty in obtaining write to:—
Chiswick Products Limited, Chiswick, London, W.4.

Woman's Home
Companion
August 1933   *Fifteen Cents in Canada*   *Ten Cents*

Is the cat on this magazine cover piecing together a puzzle picturing dogs—or methodically pawing it apart? Such whimsical illustrations characterized many magazine covers in the early and middle years of this century— and *Woman's Home Companion* was no exception. It was a popular women's magazine that began in 1897 and grew in circulation through the late 1800s and well into the 1900s. The changing life-styles of its readers and its own financial difficulties over several decades contributed to its demise. The last issue appeared in January 1957.

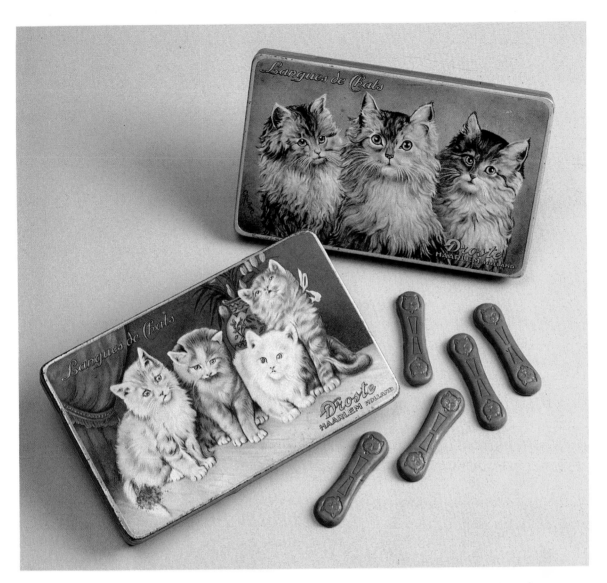

Cats adorned these candy tins from the Droste Candy Company during the 1920s and 1930s. Inside were popular chocolates called "Langues des Chats" (Cats' Tongues), so named because of their shape! Gerald Droste, Jr., began his company in Holland as a café in 1868, where he served hot chocolate. Chocolate originated in the Americas and, at the time Droste began experimenting with it, was still a relatively new and fascinating delicacy in Europe. "Langues des Chats" are no longer sold, but rich Droste chocolate is today highly acclaimed all over the world.

Almost every cat can be trained not to scratch the furniture, but some homemakers prefer that pets not even sit on a favorite chair, sofa, or rug. So companies have been experimenting with pet-repellent products for at least fifty years, as shown by this 1930s trial-size tin of Pussy Scat powder made by Sudbury Laboratories. The product did not sell well and was abandoned. Until the 1980s, Sudbury manufactured lawn, garden, and marine supplies in addition to some other pet-related products.

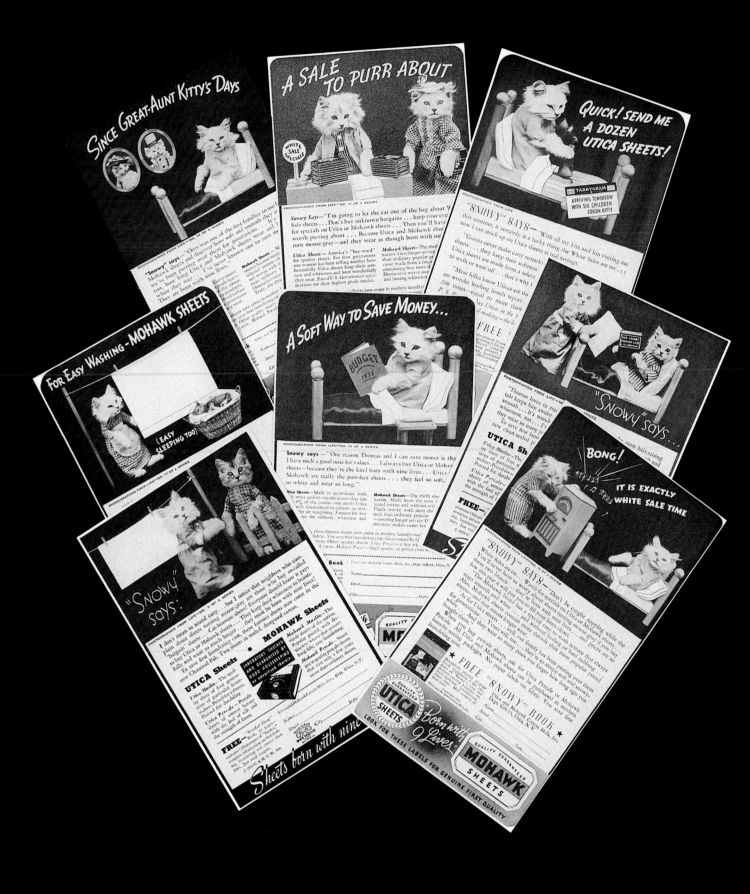

Snowy the kitten made a lasting impression on people and helped make Mohawk and Utica sheets familiar brand names in the 1930s and 1940s. The fluffy spokescat for Utica and Mohawk Cotton Mills was photographed by Harry Whittier Frees, whose popular dressed-up cats and kittens appeared on hundreds of postcards and in a number of books between 1905 and the early 1940s. Frees is said to have used kindness and patience to coax his little pets into willingly posing in miniature clothes, which were made by his mother. Frees retired from his photography business in 1942 and died in 1953.

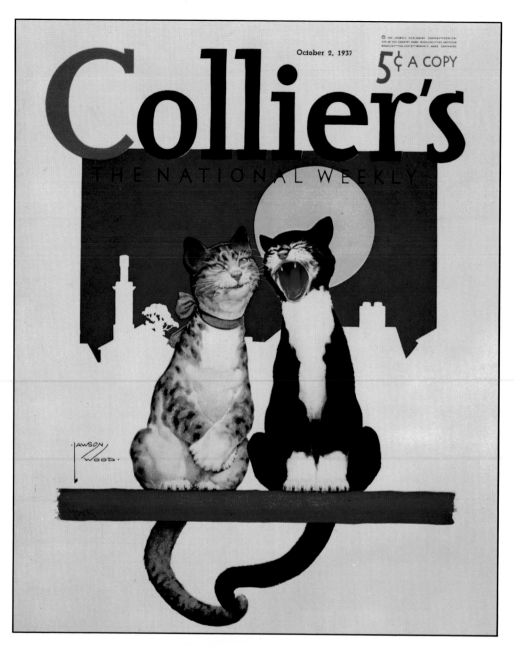

Evening feline serenades were illustrated by many nineteenth- and twentieth-century artists. *Collier's* was a popular general-interest magazine and, during the 1930s, many of its covers featured animals drawn by British artist Lawson Wood. Although Wood's illustrations accurately and wittily reflected scenes from American life—and widely appeared on calendars and magazine covers—he steadfastly refused to move to the United States. Some of his most famous art was a series of scenes featuring a chimpanzee family dressed in human clothing. P. F. Collier started his first magazine in 1888, and the last issue of *Collier's* appeared in 1957.

The words of the 1927 song "Cat-Tails" ask what any child might ask about those familiar cattail weeds—whether they might ever grow up to be pussy cats. The charming illustration on the cover of the "Cat-Tails" sheet music was drawn by Grace G. Drayton, an artist who is best known for her drawings of cherubic children. Drayton's work appeared in advertising—especially for Campbell's soups (the Campbell Kids)—and on postcards, paper dolls, and a variety of merchandise. She also drew comic strips and illustrated books until her death in 1935.

In England, Le Chat d'Or (The Golden Cat) name stood for fine chocolates as early as 1916 and began appearing in America in 1938. The advertisement at the right appeared in the British magazine *Punch* in 1931. Savon Le Chat (The Cat Soap) was unusual because the cat appeared on the soap bars themselves, in addition to the product package. The soap was made in France as early as 1834 and was prominent during the Victorian era. Today, it is the number-one soap in the French marketplace, but most of the packaging and bars no longer picture cats. Those shown here are from the 1930s.

CHOCOLATS
Le Chat d'Or
(GOLDEN CAT)

You will find Chocolats Le Chat d'Or a very correct answer to the 'present' problem during the coming Christmas Season.

The Sandhurst Assortment

To ask for a mere box of chocolates is to confess yourself a timid amateur. To demand a box of Chocolats Le Chat d'Or is to proclaim yourself a proud connoisseur . . . One who knows not only the flavour and texture of the richest chocolate, but also appreciates those subtleties of filling which make Chocolats Le Chat d'Or the envy of rival chocolatiers and the delight of those whose taste is both enterprising and unspoiled.

The Oxford and the Cambridge Assortments both at 5/- per lb. The Sandhurst at 4/6 and the Harrow at 4/-. All packed in 1, 2, & 4 lb. boxes. ¶ Obtainable from over 2,000 of the best Confectioners, or sent direct, post paid, on receipt of P.O. Please name your usual Confectioner.

CHOCOLATS LE CHAT D'OR
62 and 63 Burlington Arcade, London, W.1 (Regent 0203)

CVS—20

These children's games of the 1930s—while still colorful and fun to play—began to reflect the growing trend toward simplicity in artistic style. To play the Michigan Kitty game from the Transogram Company, players needed to understand a similar card game called Michigan rummy. Kitty Kat Cup Ball, from the Rosebud Art Company, was a game of skill. Players scored points if they flipped colored balls through the baskets tied around the cats' necks—and the balls landed in target holes. A "Kitty Kat" was scored if a player succeeded in getting three balls consecutively through the neck-baskets.

Colorful labels helped fruit growers make their brands appealing to the public. The Angora orange crate label is from about 1925. Both the associations listed on the label date to the turn of the century, when a number of such groups were formed to help growers market their crops and receive a fair price for them. Crated fruit was shipped nationwide by rail during this period. Today, the wooden crates have been replaced, for the most part, with cardboard boxes, and shipping to remote locations is routine by air express.

The 1920s were boom years for small businesses, and several canneries showed creativity with unusual label designs. The cats certainly called attention to these vegetable products—Sweet Kernel corn from Illinois, Mischief and Takme peas from Minnesota, and Chef Fancy peas from Ohio. Of course, cats also promoted the sale of cat food during the 1920s and 1930s but, at this time, cat food did not occupy a large space on grocers' shelves. Most urban cat owners fed their pets table scraps—and rural cats survived primarily on mice found on farms and in fields. The Kanna brand could be found in Arizona, C-A-T in California, and Speak-for-It in Massachusetts and California.

Felix the Cat began his career as a cartoon character in 1920 and quickly became an animated silent screen star. He was actually drawn by the little-known cartoonist Otto Messmer, who worked under the direction of Pat Sullivan at Paramount Studios, but it was Sullivan who shared the limelight with Felix throughout the years. With the advent of movies with sound, Felix's following declined, but he still managed to make millions of people laugh in comic strips, comic books, and on a variety of Felix collectibles, which are enjoying a resurgence in popularity today. This sheet music is from 1928.

More than half a century after this smiling cat first appeared on advertising trade cards for patent medicines, it gave smokers a chuckle on this cigar box. The blue eagle on the box lid shows that this brand of cigars was sold during the Depression years of 1933–35. The eagle was the symbol of the National Recovery Administration, the organization formed by President Franklin D. Roosevelt to create and administer "fair business practices." The NRA symbol was displayed and affixed to various kinds of goods from June 1933 until the Supreme Court declared the agency unconstitutional in May 1935.

The Hoffmann's Starch cats have been well known in Europe for a hundred years, but are somewhat of a curiosity in the United States. Hoffmann's, a German company, began making starch in 1876, with the cat as its corporate symbol, and the firm has retained the cat to this day. In fact, large neon cats even stand atop Hoffmann's corporate headquarters building. The colorfully lithographed tin starch box *(bottom right)* dates to the 1920s and is approximately six inches square. The wooden "trunk" *(below)* was used to transport shipments of small starch packages around 1930 and measures 20″ x 11″ x 10″. Stand-up cardboard cats *(top right)* were packed inside starch boxes as premiums as early as 1880; the examples shown here are probably from the 1950s. The starch was exported to many countries, including England, Holland, France, and Poland.

The Forties, Fifties, and Sixties

So much has happened in the last three decades it's hard to believe only thirty years have passed. From 1969, you look back and it seems like a very long time since America was at war overseas—since rationing was a way of life. But it happened just a few years ago, in the 1940s.

You've seen the development of a whole new world, filled with labor-saving devices. You saw newsreels at the movies a long time ago, but now you can see across the world in living color by simply turning on your television. Nearly everyone has at least one—and you have direct-dial telephones as well, along with a blender in the kitchen and a refrigerator that keeps food cold by electricity instead of with a huge block of ice.

You also have two cars—a station wagon and a luxury sedan in your driveway—and you can open your garage door by remote control. The new interstate highway system links distant cities around the country, but it signals the death of many small-town businesses. Now, traffic whizzes past town on a bypass that has a number instead of a name.

At the theater, you've seen some wonderful plays—*A Streetcar Named Desire* in the forties; *The King and I* and *Cat on a Hot Tin Roof* in the fifties and, not too long ago, a new sensation, *Hello, Dolly! Casablanca* was your favorite movie in 1942 and you've managed to see it a half-dozen times since then, along with *From Here to Eternity, West Side Story,* and *My Fair Lady.*

You've seen society question itself and the status quo. You've lived through spy scares, Korea, and now there's Vietnam. You've wept for a slain president, thrilled to the launching of satellites and men into space, watched rock and roll revolutionize the music industry, noticed skirt hems steadily rise to an astounding shortness, and flown across the country in a matter of hours in jet airplanes.

Sometimes you wonder if this is the culmination of our ability to achieve—or just the beginning. Luckily for you, your cat doesn't care at all about such lofty philosophy—just the present, as you thoughtfully stroke its soft fur and enjoy a grateful purr in response.

A fastidiously clean cat helped illustrate the advertising line for Fleetwood cigarettes: "Every puff cleans itself." The advertisement at right appeared in magazines in 1943. The following year, the Axton-Fisher Tobacco Company became part of the Phillip Morris Co., one of the nation's largest cigarette manufacturers.

Every puff of Fleetwood smoke Cleans Itself!

In the smoke of Fleetwoods you get *less* nicotine, *less* throat irritants, and *less* of the tars that stain fingers and teeth ... provided you do not smoke Fleetwoods farther than old-size cigarettes ... because the smoke is *filtered cleaner* by being drawn through more tobacco, 20% more for the first puff and 50% more for the last puff. You are invited to try *a cleaner, finer smoke.*

FLEETWOOD
A CLEANER, FINER SMOKE

A SUPERIOR CIGARETTE AT THE STANDARD PRICE • THE AXTON-FISHER TOBACCO COMPANY, INC. • "HOUSE OF TRADITION" • LOUISVILLE, KY.

Peake's Favorite Pin-up Girl

"At the service of the country". . . *This phrase, true of the railroads in peacetime, is more than ever true today, when all railroad facilities are working overtime, carrying the hugest load in history. While C & O is doing its level best to handle essential civilian needs, wartime traffic . . . of necessity . . . comes first. Aware of that, we are confident that Chessie's many admirers will understand her occasional inability to be the same helpful kitten she was in days gone by. It won't be too long, she hopes, before she can be her old self again. Meanwhile, she's doing all she can to bring that day nearer.*

Chesapeake and Ohio

CHESAPEAKE AND OHIO RAILWAY

During World War II, many American companies incorporated patriotic themes into their advertising. The Chesapeake & Ohio Railway's annual calendar for 1944 (left) showed the company's mascot ("Chessie") as a pin-up girl for her husband ("Peake")—a soldier away at war. Chessie was originally introduced in the 1930s to illustrate the "Sleep like a Kitten" slogan for the company's air-conditioned sleeping coaches.

Rationing and "doing without" were facts of everyday life in wartime America. The Hastings Manufacturing Company promoted their automobile piston rings in the 1945 ad shown at right as an aid to extending the engine life of cars people owned during the war years.

The Corticelli kitten donned a soldier's uniform and marched across America on every spool of Belcort thread produced during the war. A kitten was used as the symbol of Corticelli silk thread from the turn of the century, but when silk was unavailable during the war the company introduced Belcort—a quadrolastic processed cotton thread—as a substitute. Belding Heminway Company, Inc., continues to utilize kittens in its marketing and as a corporate symbol to this day.

How many lives has an engine?

The cat-of-nine-lives has nothing on the automobile engine. Its one life can be stretched and stretched — long beyond our pre-war beliefs. All it takes is attention, and the prompt replacement of worn parts.

Among the parts you must watch are the piston rings. They take a beating in any engine, and they last a long time. But when they do wear out they must be replaced

promptly to protect the cylinder walls and other vital parts.

At the very first sign of ring wear—smoke, oil-pumping or loss of power—it will pay you to get Hastings piston rings. They *stop* oil-pumping, *check* cylinder wear and *restore* performance. Ask any motor specialist.

HASTINGS MANUFACTURING COMPANY · HASTINGS, MICHIGAN
Hastings Mfg. of Canada, Ltd., Toronto

Tough..but oh so gentle

HASTINGS STEEL-VENT PISTON RINGS
*Tough on oil-pumping · Gentle on cylinder walls

A skittish kitten drew attention to Imperial Whiskey in this 1943 magazine advertisement from Hiram Walker & Sons, Ltd. If the charming style of this illustration looks familiar, compare it with the ad for Fleetwood cigarettes on page 71. Both illustrations are by the same artist, Albert Staehle, whose sensitive and humorous depiction of animals appeared in many ads during the 1940s and 1950s, as well as in a long-running series of magazine covers for the *Saturday Evening Post* featuring a cocker spaniel that constantly got into trouble.

Playful cats in the late 1940s could have wished for catnip in their holiday dreams and, if they were good, they may have been lucky enough to receive a package of Vo-Toys dried catnip leaves. These packages were produced for the 1947 Christmas season as holiday "stocking stuffers" for cats. Vo-Toys, Inc., was founded in 1940 by German immigrant Kurt Vogel. During World War II, catnip was hard to obtain so production ceased; after the war, the line of products expanded until the company now produces almost six thousand items for cats, dogs, birds, hamsters, and other small pets.

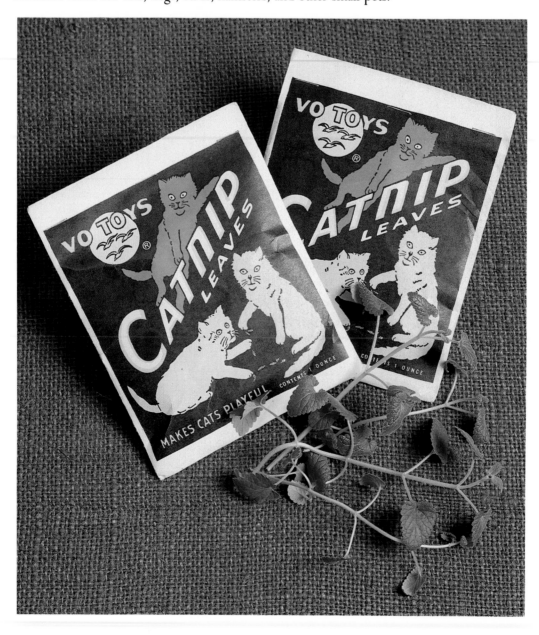

You wouldn't want a bristling whiskey!
That's why Imperial is *"velveted"*

This "Velveting" is what makes IMPERIAL so gentle to your taste. For velveting works wonders in smoothness—gives IMPERIAL the easy-to-take goodness which is making millions say "wonderful!" And—a goodness that makes IMPERIAL one of America's most-wanted whiskies.

But like sugar and coffee, IMPERIAL is on quota—because our stills are now making war alcohol instead of whiskey.

And sometimes delivery is held up a day or so because shipments of war materials and food naturally come first.

So if your store or tavern sometimes cannot supply you with IMPERIAL, please be patient and remember there is a mighty good reason for it.

A blend. Eighty-six proof. 70% grain neutral spirits. Copr. 1943, Hiram Walker & Sons Inc., Peoria, Illinois.

IMPERIAL
REG. U.S. PAT. OFF.

The *"velveted"* whiskey

Advertising for Chatham blankets featured a kitten in magazines of the 1950s and 1960s. The blankets themselves were named "Purrey" because of their kitten-like softness. The Chatham Manufacturing Company, which was founded in 1877 as Elkin Woolen Mills in Elkin, North Carolina, has produced fine fabrics and woolen products ever since.

CHATHAM *Purrey* BLANKET

...warmer than blankets nearly twice the price

Chatham Blankets America

NEWS! "Purrey"*, America's most popular blanket, now comes in summer and winter weights

Puss 'N Boots was one of the first brands of cat food for which a major national advertising campaign was launched. Taking its name from the fabled children's story, Puss 'N Boots was introduced in 1934 by the Coast Fishing Company. The Quaker Oats Company purchased Puss 'N Boots in 1950, and the magazine advertisement shown above appeared the next year. It's an unusual ad because it featured several calico cats; most feline advertising stars are solid-colored. Quaker is better known for its breakfast cereals but still produces Puss 'N Boots.

Dr. Scat-O-Fone was introduced around 1950 as a disinfectant for cleaning telephone mouthpieces, and these unusual bottles can still be found today. The product was especially popular in offices where several people shared a telephone because once Dr. Scat-O-Fone was used on the mouthpiece, the phone had a clean, fresh scent. The Dr. Scat Chemical Company has been making typewriter cleaners and private label products since 1930.

A strikingly mysterious cat created an unusual and memorable advertisement for My Sin perfume in 1962. This provocative scent was a 1925 creation of Jeanne Lanvin, a prominent French designer. It was named My Sin to honor her illegitimate daughter, Marie-Blanche, and is a blend of some of the rarest and most expensive floral essences available in the 1920s—lily of the valley, lilac, jonquil, mock-orange (syringa), and heliotrope. My Sin has endured in the hotly competitive fragrance industry and can still be purchased, but nearly a quarter of a century has passed since cats have been seen endorsing it.

MY SIN

...a most provocative perfume!

LANVIN

Purse size $3; Spray Mist $5;
Toilet Water from $3; (plus tax)

Purrr-fect Performance!

ALERTNESS of a kitten . . . lightning-fast starts, rapid warm-up, ever-so-smooth power! That's what you get with the superior *Fire-Power* of Texaco Fire-Chief gasoline. Try some today. At Texaco Dealers everywhere.

TEXACO *FIRE-CHIEF* GASOLINE

TEXACO DEALERS

where you get . . .

SKY CHIEF GASOLINE

FIRE-CHIEF GASOLINE

HAVOLINE AND TEXACO MOTOR OILS

MARFAK LUBRICATION

TEXACO

THE TEXAS COMPANY

TUNE IN . . . Texaco Star Theatre presents the new Eddie Bracken show every Sunday night.   See newspapers for time and station.

For over a decade, animals promoted Texaco gasoline—including the kitten shown above from 1946, and a long-running series of advertisements featuring Dalmatian puppies (usually considered firehouse dogs). Texaco originated in 1902 as The Texas Company. People used the word Texaco as a shortened form of the corporate name when sending cable messages, and it became such a popular nickname that the company itself was renamed in 1959. Fire Chief gasoline was introduced in 1932. Today, Texaco continues to produce petroleum-based products.

Lorillard, the nation's oldest tobacco company, used cute kittens to focus readers' attention on their magazine advertising in the 1950s. The fluffy white kitten appeared in 1951; the playful tabby in 1953. During this phase of tobacco's long advertising history, some cigarette manufacturers were able to obtain endorsements for their brands from doctors, giving implied medical approval. Lorillard, instead, relied on its position of leadership and expertise in producing fine tobacco. The Old Gold brand was introduced in 1926, when blends of domestic and imported tobacco were replacing the popularity of Turkish tobacco in post–World War I America. Old Gold took its name from the section of Virginia where its golden tobacco grows. The brand is still sold today.

In American folklore, black cats could mean good luck in addition to the more commonly believed bad luck of superstition and Halloween legends. The cat on the Black Cat Candles box from the King Novelty Company of Chicago, Illinois, is a good example of a happy black cat symbol. The candles were first produced in 1939 and, when this box was made in the 1960s, the candles were available in blue, green, yellow, white, red, pink, orange, and black. The candles are no longer produced.

"Woman Reading" is the title of this poster by Will Barnet, contemporary American artist. It was first created as a limited edition serigraph and then reproduced as an advertising poster in 1969 to promote an exhibition of Barnet's works. Cats and nature play an important role in Barnet's paintings and—as he did here—he often includes both his family's pet cat, Madame Butterfly, and his wife in poster creations. Madame Butterfly is actually a calico cat but because Barnet exercises artistic license, she often appears in a color that complements the work as a whole rather than in her natural multicolor state!

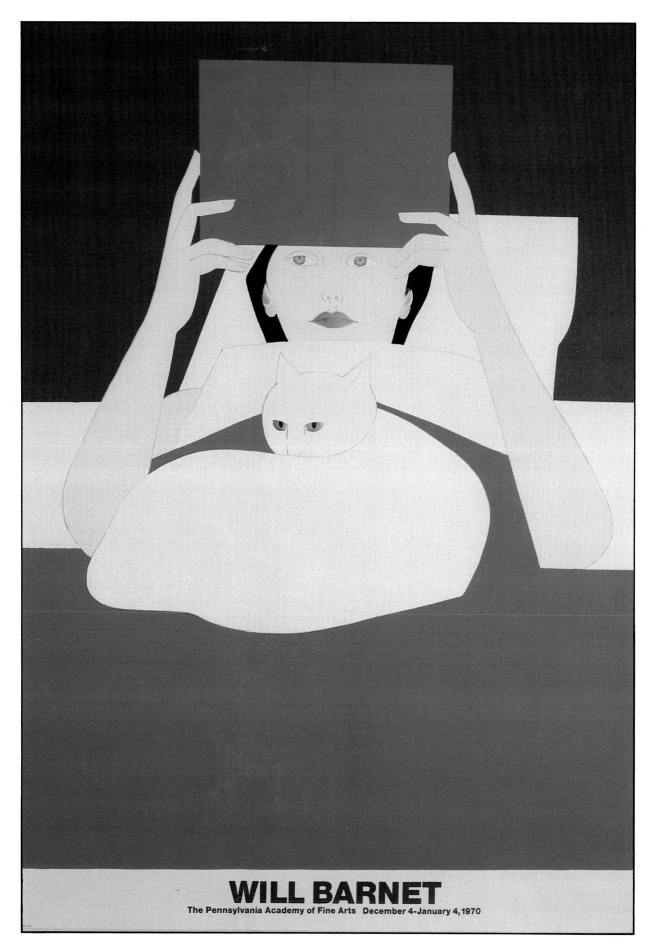

WILL BARNET
The Pennsylvania Academy of Fine Arts   December 4-January 4, 1970

1970 to the Present

t's the eighties. In fact, you went through 1984 with scarcely more than a passing thought about the book of the same name—with all its dire predictions.

Now it's the day of the entrepreneur and the computer age. You have digital clocks, telephone answering machines, a stereo system, and a videocassette recorder that lets you watch movies at home without commercial interruptions. (Of course, you still watch TV, and always notice the advertisements that feature cats!) All the magazine ads are in color, with photography generally replacing artists' illustrations.

Stores are filled with convenience foods and electronic gadgets. No longer must people work in jobs that are strictly stereotyped for men or women. This must be the future, you think.

It would be easy to take all this for granted —the fine standard of living you enjoy and the advances made in medicine and science. But you've also lived with more somber thoughts of concern for the environment and where technology and big business may lead us. You do your part to conserve resources while you hope that peace will be our way of life forever.

You've worn everything from T-shirts with jeans to designer suits. Eaten everything from crepes to quiche—with a fairly large number of hot dogs, burgers, and fries in between. You've seen drive-in restaurants mature into fast-food chains and drive-in theaters come and go. When it's hot, you always have air conditioning; when it snows, the streets are cleaned by giant snowplows and you snuggle under an electric blanket.

You have plenty of credit cards, you exercise regularly, and one of your favorite movies in the last few years was about a fantasy cat from outer space!

The eighties have seen long-dormant volcanoes spray orange lava into the clouds, sleeping nations jolted awake by earthquakes, and Halley's comet make a streaking return engagement to the evening skies (though it wasn't as spectacular as when you saw it in 1910). You've seen famine and political unrest around the world. But you've also seen the beginnings of a return to classic values and a new humane concern for suffering people everywhere and for the animals that share our world.

You realize you're on the brink of another turn of the century. In a society with such sophistication, you think the world could use a link with the past, something that puts it all in perspective. Thank goodness some things never change—there will always be cats!

After years of promoting cigars and cigarettes by their appearances on boxes, labels, packages, and advertisements, cats finally were able to present the opposition viewpoint when this poster was introduced in 1983. Brandt Bralds, who came to America from the Netherlands in 1980, created the cats of this unusual eight-color lithograph. It was produced by Bo-Tree Productions, Palo Alto, California, in cooperation with the American Lung Association. The poster is still available and a portion of the proceeds of each sale is donated to the association.

WE DON'T WANT YOU TO SMOKE.

YOUR FURRY FRIENDS DON'T WANT YOU TO SMOKE. YOUR LUNG ASSOCIATION DOESN'T WANT YOU TO SMOKE. THAT'S WHY
THIS POSTER WAS CREATED. WE PLACED IT HERE BECAUSE WE DON'T WANT YOU TO SMOKE EITHER. ESPECIALLY HERE. ✝ ✝ ✝

Dubonnet, a spicy, sweet wine aperitif, has been produced in France since 1846. Much of Dubonnet's early advertising featured a cat, as did the label on its bottles. The bottles shown here are from 1985, but Dubonnet has been sold in the United States since 1933, when Prohibition ended. Over 150,000 cases of Dubonnet are sold annually.

The 1977 Neiman-Marcus Christmas Book featured "T.J." the cat on its cover, a contemporary illustration by American artist Paul Davis. The cat played a key role in the company's fiftieth anniversary holiday festivities— T.J.'s image was emblazoned on the sides of a corporate jet and a real-life T.J. accompanied Neiman-Marcus executives in the plane on what they called the Christmas Cat Patrol. Its mission: to deliver special advance copies of the catalog to the press in cities where the company's retail stores were located. The Christmas Book was mailed to 1.6 million people that year.

Neiman-Marcus was founded in 1907 in Dallas, Texas, and quickly became one of the nation's most respected and fashionable department stores. The Neiman-Marcus Christmas Book is world famous as a fabulous holiday catalog featuring distinctive gifts. Today, Neiman-Marcus has stores across America and is a division of Carter Hawley Hale Stores, Inc.

"The cat that doesn't act finicky, soon loses control of his owner."

Says Morris, 9-Lives® spokesman and TV personality.

"I think every cat should act finicky. It helps reinforce that imperious reputation.

"But it's tough putting on an act when your owner serves up 9-Lives. Such temptation. Such variety. Such nutrition. It's more than mere fur and bones can stand.

"My willpower goes kaput with 9-Lives Kitty Burgers. Like Chicken. Or Chicken and Liver. Or Chicken and Kidney.

"And I really double-time to my dish when I'm served 9-Lives Tuna. Or Tuna and Chicken. Or Tuna and Liver.

"Of course, one nice thing about acting finicky is that it feels so good when you stop."

© 1969 STAR-KIST FOODS, INC.

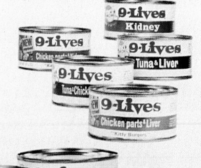

9-Lives...the nutritious foods cats really like. Even Morris.

Morris is probably the most famous cat in advertising. He is the eccentric spokescat for 9-Lives cat food, made by Star-Kist Foods, Inc., and was actually "discovered" in an animal shelter. He skyrocketed to fame as the star of numerous television commercials and printed advertisements, and his picture appears on the 9-Lives packaging as well. This 1969 ad explains his "finicky eater" philosophy which has been the company's successful selling strategy for the last seventeen years. Morris also endorses June as Adopt-a-Cat Month in cooperation with animal shelters nationwide. Although the original Morris passed on to his heavenly reward (of eternal 9-Lives, he might have said!) in 1978, his spirit lives on through a carefully selected orange lookalike.

"Kitty," the cat on the cover of this record album, was painted by American artist George White around 1821, but its folk art style is appropriate for this modern folk/bluegrass album from Rounder Records. Rounder specializes in producing and distributing "roots music" albums—sounds that are traditionally based or ethnic in origin—such as blues, folk, mountain, bluegrass, Cajun, reggae, Celtic, and African. Buddy Thomas (that's his picture on the record label) played banjo and fiddle music from his Kentucky heritage on this album, which featured his specially arranged version of an old country tune called "Kitty Puss." Thomas died at age thirty-nine, shortly before this album was released in 1970, the year Rounder Records was founded. Today, the company sells more than a million albums each year.

Pirate cats unearthing a treasure chest of
ice cream made a strikingly creative
statement for Dean's ice cream in this
advertising poster from 1976. It was one of
a series of posters in which animals donned
clothes and were given human attributes—
to dramatize the pleasures of eating Dean's
ice cream. Other animals in the series
included lions, monkeys, and a duck.
Dean's ice cream has been produced since
1947 by Dean Foods, Inc., Franklin Park,
Illinois. The company was founded in 1925
in Pecatonica, Illinois.

Dean's All Yo

Discover the flavors of
grocer's freezer. Dean's e
Naturally. At Dean's e
whole Grade A milk and

ce Cream Dreams Come True

many paces as you need to your
rs. And you'll treasure every one.
tural flavor. We start with fresh,
ng but the best. And come up with

gems like Strawberry Cheesecake. Rich, natural cheesecake ice cream with
ribbons of fresh strawberry throughout. And with all the country goodness
you expect from Dean's. Incredible! So the next time you have a taste for the
thrill of adventure, dig into Dean's. It's enough to get any captain hooked.

You just know it's McCall's.

"Cats like safe hiding places for looking out on the world." McCall's collared animal psychologist/veterinarian Dr. Michael Fox for his light-hearted, sure-footed analysis of mischievous kittens, jealous dogs, amorous budgies and other pet quirks—every month, in "Understanding Your Pet." Whether it's pets or people: the approach is lively; the graphics, unmatched; the signature, McCall's.

McCall's. You just know it's for you.

This magazine advertisement had a double purpose—stimulating readership of *McCall's* magazine and promoting advertising revenues. It appeared in *Advertising Age,* a trade journal for people in the advertising business, in 1979. *McCall's* dates back to 1876, when James McCall and his wife began publishing a small four-page magazine (on pink paper) to promote a line of ladies' dress patterns they had developed. Originally called *The Queen,* the magazine gradually added fiction and various articles of interest to women until, in the 1930s, *McCall's* magazine became the first women's magazine to reach a circulation of one million copies per issue. From World War II to the present, the magazine has continued to reflect women's attitudes and life-styles and, today, *McCall's* has more than five million readers a month.

"Gold Standard" is a 1985 advertisement for Eastman Kodak Company, the firm that has made taking pictures as easy as pressing a button. The founder of the company, George Eastman, was a young bank clerk when he first became interested in photography, around 1877. Although photography was already about fifty years old then, it was used almost exclusively by professionals because of the need for complicated and cumbersome equipment. Eastman developed breakthroughs in the field—including film in rolls (1884) and a lightweight camera, the No. 1 Kodak (1888). This portable camera cost $25 and came loaded with film for 100 exposures. Once the pictures were taken, people sent their cameras to Eastman's company in Rochester, New York. There the film was developed, prints were made, new film was installed, and the cameras were shipped back to their owners. Today, Eastman Kodak Company is a world leader in the photographic industry. Incidentally, the word "Kodak" has no particular meaning. Eastman made it up in 1888 because he liked the letter "k." He experimented with various letter combinations until he found a word (and sound) that he liked.

200 mm at 1/60 sec at f/32

How to reach the gold standard.

So close. And yet so far. The object of your desires is within reach with Kodacolor VR 200 film. Sensitive enough to make the most brilliant colors shine. Sharp enough to capture small details. Fast enough to catch your subject as it darts through the shadows. And so versatile that even in shifting light, a golden opportunity won't slip away.

Kodak film. Because time goes by.

The newest addition to Movado's incomparable
9-Ligne Quartz collection. Ultra-slim. 14 karat gold
integrated bracelet and dial with sapphire crystal.
Accurate to within 60 seconds per year.

MOVADO

A century of Swiss watchcraft. 1881-1981

Fine watches bearing the Movado name have been made in picturesque
Switzerland for over a hundred years. One of the company's distinctions
is that, in the 1970s, a Movado watch was honored for excellence in
modern design and became part of the permanent collection of the
Museum of Contemporary Art in New York City. The black cat was
used in a series of Movado magazine advertisements in the early 1980s.
This one appeared in 1981.

Oneida, Ltd., one of the world's largest producers of silver products, appropriately used a silver tabby kitten in
this advertising poster of the early 1980s. The company is probably best known for its silverplated tableware
called Community Plate, a product name that reflects an interesting corporate history. The successful silver
products company grew from an experimental religious and social community—the Oneida Community—
founded in 1848. The Community was dissolved by its own members in 1880, but Oneida, Ltd., still
has its headquarters on the original communal grounds in Oneida, New York. The company has often
used animals to add warmth and appeal to its advertising over the years and has made its advertising
posters available to the public.

This "conductor cat" appeared in 1983 on signs in record shop windows and in displays that promoted the album *Classical Cats.* The record, which featured the same design on the album cover, was produced by London Records, Inc.

Acknowledgments

We would like to thank the people who helped us in the creation of
The Cat Sold It!

Ken Kapson, who generously gave of his time, advice, and ideas, and who enthusiastically shared with us his advertising expertise, creativity, and perspective of the past to enrich this endeavor; Jane Jordan Browne, who encouraged us and represents us; and Brandt Aymar, editor at Crown Publishers, Inc., who has continued to recognize the importance of the cat in advertising as an interesting link between past and present and who helped us share this book with others. We are also indebted to the multitude of people who carefully saved the cats pictured here. Because of their sentimentality, these beautiful felines have survived the passing of many years to be rediscovered and, therefore, appreciated today.

We also thank the many companies that granted permission to reproduce their advertising, including: COVER AND TITLE PAGE ILLUSTRATION: Belding Heminway Company, Inc. This kitten is a registered trademark and is reprinted with the permission of Belding Heminway Company, Inc. All rights reserved. (9) Used with permission from Parker Brothers. (10) Garland Commercial Industries, Inc., a Welbilt Company, Freeland, Pennsylvania. (21) Courtesy, Chappell Music Limited. (32) Courtesy, Nabisco Brands, Inc. (38–40) The Three Little Kittens, Game of Puss, and Pussy Ring Game are games of

Milton Bradley Company and are reproduced with the permission of the owner. (48) Reproduced by courtesy of Reckitt & Colman Products Limited. (53) Reproduced by courtesy of Reckitt & Colman Products Limited. (55-top) Used by permission of Droste USA Ltd. (56–57) Used by permission of J. P. Stevens & Co., Inc. UTICA is a registered trademark of J. P. Stevens & Co., Inc. (67) Copyright 1928 and © 1956 by Sam Fox Publishing Co., Inc., New York, New York. Used by permission. (72) Chessie and Peake are registered trademarks of Chessie System Railroads and are used with the company's permission. (73-bottom) Belding Heminway Company, Inc. (80) Courtesy of Texaco, Inc. (83) Copyright, Will Barnet, 1970. Commissioned by Poster Originals, Ltd. (87) Permission granted by Neiman-Marcus. (88) Copyright © 1969 Star-Kist Foods, Inc. Used by permission of Star-Kist Foods, Inc., and Leo Burnett Company, Inc. (89) Courtesy of Rounder Records. (92) Reprinted by permission of the McCall Publishing Company. (93) Reprinted courtesy of Eastman Kodak Company.

Every effort has been made to contact the copyright and trademark owners or their representatives. If there have been any omissions, please notify us and we will rectify them in future printings.